A Walk Across America

Bill Holden

Contents

Rigby

A Harcourt Achieve Imprint

www.Rigby.com

1-800-531-5015

Intoducing Bill Holden

My name is Bill Holden, and I WALKED ACROSS AMERICA—from Arizona to Chicago, a distance of 2,100 miles, in 172 days. Many people said it couldn't be done by a 56-year-old man with sore knees, but I proved them wrong.

I've been a teacher and a coach for 32 years. I'm also a proud father of a son, Josh, and a daughter, Becky. And through thick and thin, I'm a Chicago Cubs fan!

My kids, Josh and Becky, cheered me on while I set off to walk across America.

Growing up in Chicago in the 1950s, I watched Cubs games on a black-and-white television and saw my first Cubs game at Wrigley Field for my ninth birthday in 1957. The Cubs lost a double-header, but I was hooked nonetheless.

When an infielder named Ernie Banks joined the Cubs, I began forming a philosophy about life from watching him: Don't give up; look for the best in people; don't worry about what others think of you; and enjoy every day because life is too short to not have fun!

CUBS

ERNIE BANKS

1st Base

In 1960 Ron Santo, a rookie third baseman, joined the team, and he, like Ernie Banks, always had time for the fans. Early in Santo's career, I managed to get down to the Cubs' dugout with a friend, and when we peered around the corner, there was Ron Santo furiously eating candy bars. We thought maybe he had skipped breakfast, but the Cubs' batboy explained that Santo was a diabetic, which we knew nothing about at the time.

What Is Diabetes?

Diabetes is a disease in which your blood sugar levels are higher than they should be. A lot of the food we eat is turned into sugar, or glucose, to give us energy. The pancreas is an organ in our body near the stomach which makes something called insulin. Insulin helps the sugar get into your body's cells. When you have diabetes, your body can't make enough insulin or it doesn't use the insulin properly. This causes too much sugar in your blood. Diabetes can cause blindness, kidney failure, heart disease, and other things. Diabetes is the sixth leading cause of death in the United States.

CUBS

RON SANTO   3rd Base

During the early 1960s, I got to meet Ron Santo. He signed autographs at Gromer's Supermarket in Elgin, Illinois. As the local newsboy, I was in Gromer's nearly every day selling my newspapers.

That snowy, cold January day, I trudged through the thick blanket of snow delivering newspapers as fast as I could, and then I headed to Gromer's to meet my hero.

The harsh wind blew me through the doors of the store, and there he was—Ron Santo! No one else was in the store . . . except me and a few employees!

The weather was so bad that few people had left their homes. So there we stood: the young, husky third baseman and the skinny newsboy. I dug into my coat pocket and pulled out the candy bar I'd been saving for him.

A big smile crossed Santo's face as I handed it to him. He thanked me and told me it would come in handy. For the next hour I made small talk with Ron Santo, my hero, while every once in a while a customer would blow in from the frigid outdoors and he'd sign an autograph. Before long I headed home for dinner. Santo thanked me again for the candy bar as I walked out.

A Dream Unfolds

Ron Santo retired from baseball in 1974 and went on to become a radio broadcaster. Then, in 2001, he had a leg amputated because of complications from diabetes. In 2002 he lost his second leg because of diabetes. Chicago Cubs fans everywhere were concerned about their favorite former third baseman.

In 2003, when I taught on a Native American Reservation near Phoenix, Arizona, I saw many kids and adults afflicted with diabetes—there were kids with thick glasses whose eyesight had been affected by the disease, and sometimes a student would nod off in the middle of class or miss an entire week of school because of diabetes. I saw amputees on the reservation, too, and I wondered how I could help.

Diabetes can cause people to have poor eyesight. Often eyeglasses are needed to help diabetics.

On New Year's Eve 2005, my son, Josh, gave me a copy of *This Old Cub*, a movie based on Ron Santo's life. I watched it many times, reliving the moments of Ron Santo as a young ballplayer, clicking his heels in mid-air when the Cubs won. And now he was struggling with his artificial legs but always keeping a positive attitude. Suddenly a dream started to unfold—to walk across the country, spreading Ron Santo's story and the stories of the diabetics on the reservation.

Ron Santo played third base for the Chicago Cubs from 1960-1973.

When I told my friend of 30 years, Greg Reisig, about my plan, he said, "You must be joking! From Arizona to Chicago?"

Greg knew by my voice that I was serious, and as I walked, Greg would be an important part of my team—my cheerleader from afar.

Then when I called the Juvenile Diabetes Research Foundation (JDRF) to share my plan to raise money for the foundation, the woman I talked to was speechless before she asked, "Are you sure about this? That's an awful long walk!"

I told her, "I'll make it!"

Next I called my old college roommate, Mike Murphy, a sports talk show host on WSCR radio in Chicago. He put me in touch with Ron and his family and things started falling into place.

I told Jeff Santo, Ron's son and the filmmaker of *This Old Cub*, that I didn't want any support vehicles following me. Before long, Jeff was setting up hotels and meals on my route. We set a fundraising goal of $250,000 for JDRF.

JDRF and Its Walks

"Walks" and JDRF have a strong relationship, and Ron Santo has been an important part of JDRF Walks for many years. The Walks raise funds and awareness for diabetes research. In 2005 $81 million was raised through over 200 JDRF Walks around the country. This would be the first walk across the country for JDRF.

My college roommate, Mike Murphy, put me in touch with the Santos. Murphy supported me throughout my walk.

WALK TO CURE DIABETES

JDRF Juvenile Diabetes Research Foundation International

dedicated to finding a cure

Starting Out in Arizona

Jan 11, 2005, was a crisp, cold Sunday as I began my walk. I walked down Prescott Valley, Arizona's main street carrying only a backpack. Cars honked at me because that morning Prescott's *Daily Courier* blared the headline, "Prescott Valley's Bill Holden On His Way To Wrigley Field—By Foot."

I stopped first at my daughter's apartment, giving her my backpack to take to Mayer, Arizona, about 12 miles from Prescott Valley. Because my backpack weighed nearly 20 pounds, I hoped to rely on others to take my bag from town to town for me.

Packing Only the Essentials

I packed only the essentials in my old canvas backpack:
- ☑ two sweatshirts
- ☑ four t-shirts
- ☑ four pairs of underwear
- ☑ two pairs of socks
- ☑ sweatpants
- ☑ shorts
- ☑ a light jacket
- ☑ an umbrella
- ☑ long johns
- ☑ gloves
- ☑ personal items such as soap, shampoo, and a toothbrush

I got rid of the umbrella, long johns, and gloves as the weather improved.

I stumbled into Mayer, Arizona, eight hours later, and as I reached the city limits, a van pulled up and a man stuck his head out the window, asking if I was alright. I said I was just a little tired! The couple took me into town, and as we rode the short distance, the woman asked for my autograph. That was only the first of many requests for my autograph.

Walking 12 miles from Prescott Valley to the town of Mayer, Arizona, was an eight hour walk.

On Tuesday, January 13, 2005, I was ready to set out again when a man named Roger Neuhaus introduced himself and handed me a cell phone for my trip. Roger's employer, the Verde Valley Medical Center, had donated the phone and pledged $5,000 to JDRF. Roger then took my bag down to Clear Creek, where I'd stay the night.

As I left, I felt great. I had already gotten a large donation, and I was only a few days into my walk. As I walked away, the sun was out, yet it was misting! The jagged mountains turned blue in the mist.

Bill Holden's Walk Across America

Through a misty rain, I trudged ten miles until I reached a small outpost, the Clear Creek Village Store. Roger had given the clerks my bag, and for an hour, as customers came in and out, I sat on a milk crate waiting for someone to volunteer to put me up for the night. When Landon Williams heard about my trip, he invited me to his warm, welcoming mobile home where I spent the evening listening to him talk about his family.

By 6 A.M. the next morning, with the grayness of daybreak on the horizon, I stepped onto the highway, headed for Payson, Arizona. Two days later, as I finally neared Payson, a van pulled over and a local radio station reporter asked for an interview. For 20 minutes, I visited with the people of Payson over the radio, and then I was on my own again to finish my walk into Payson. I had walked 17 miles that day.

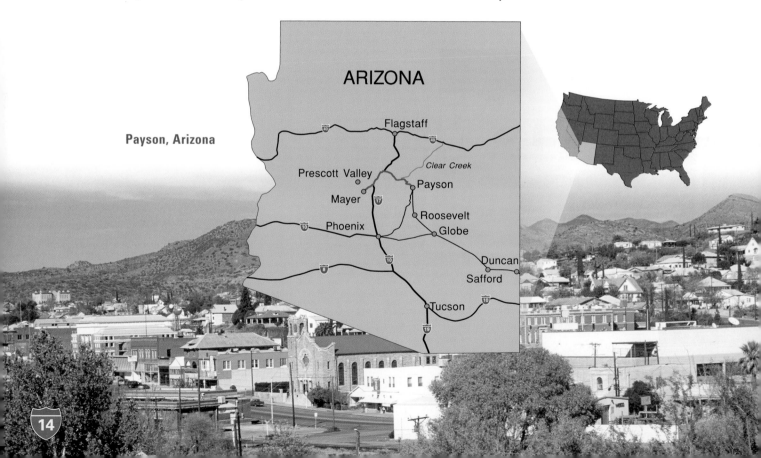

Payson, Arizona

I spent two nights in Payson doing newspaper and radio interviews, and from there I traveled through Roosevelt, Arizona, and into Globe, Arizona. I remember vividly one vehicle that stopped me. The woman driving the pickup motioned for me to open the passenger door where a man sat. The couple was Native American. When the woman pointed to the man's legs, I saw he was missing his right foot. We exchanged no words; none were needed. The woman then reached into a cooler and handed me some ice-cold orange juice. I accepted the gift and mumbled, "Thanks." This first-hand account of what diabetes had done was the reason I walked! I stared at the truck as it disappeared on the horizon.

I met many friendly people walking down Globe, Arizona's Main Street.

Onward I walked through the Arizona towns of Safford and Duncan until I reached the border between Arizona and New Mexico. I made my first crossing over a state line, and when I walked out of Arizona and into New Mexico, there suddenly was nothing to see but miles of desert. The next major town was Lordsburg, New Mexico, 50 miles away with nothing in between.

Friendly People in New Mexico

After walking ten miles, I rode with a local sheriff into Lordsburg. Here I began asking the police for help with my bag transportation and "walk-backs." In New Mexico, the next town might be 50 miles away so their help was crucial.

On the morning I left Lordsburg, I ate breakfast with a group of cowboys. They offered me a horse for the rest of the trip. I turned them down—no horse needed for this walker!

What's a "Walk Back?"

As I planned my walk, I had to think about what to do when my next destination would be more than 15 miles away. So I decided I'd just have to do a "walk-back." That meant that once I had walked my 12–15 miles a day, I could get a ride to the next town where my bag would be waiting for me. But the next day I'd get a ride back to where I left off the previous day. I was determined to walk the entire distance. This meant that I would have to rely on the spirit of the American people to help me out!

I was very thankful for the Lordsburg police, who helped me through the remote desert lands that surround Lordsburg, New Mexico.

My next stop was in Deming, New Mexico, where I stayed at the Butterfield Stage Motel. The Murray family welcomed me and took me to dinner at the best place in town, an Italian restaurant.

While I was there, I talked with a high school health class about my journey. Amazed, students asked, "Going through such desolate country, aren't you afraid?"

I told them people were always willing to help.

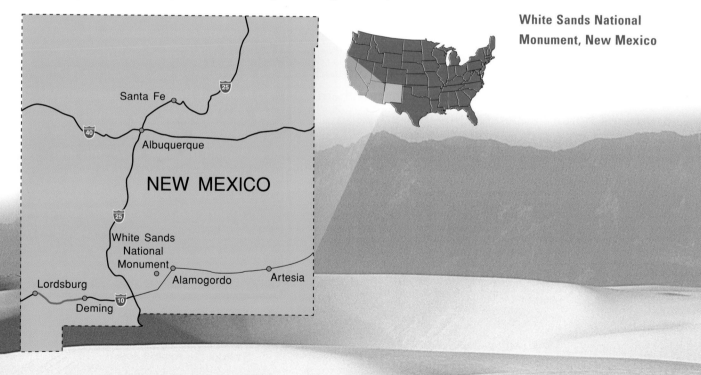

White Sands National Monument, New Mexico

Jeff Santo's crew did a great job reserving motels, and local restaurants donated fabulous meals. Days clicked by, and while my knees were sore, the pain wasn't as noticeable after a couple hours of walking. The scenery was magnificent: jagged mountain ranges rising on all horizons, sweeping low into valleys of sand and sage brush. By now my wind-burned face was bright red.

I always tried to walk facing the traffic so I could see the cars as they went by me.

In Alamogordo, New Mexico, I met up again with Roger Neuhaus, the man I met at the beginning of the trip who gave me the cell phone. He planned to walk with me for a few days. As we headed out through some of the most beautiful country in America, we quickly discovered how dangerous this beautiful country can be for a walker. The mountains came straight down to the highway, and to stay away from traffic, I had to cling to the mountain base, carefully peeking around mountainsides to see where to walk and to avoid head-on collisions with oncoming cars. There was absolutely no shoulder to walk on.

Alamogordo, New Mexico, was both a beautiful part of my walk and a dangerous part. The mountain highways gave me little room for walking alongside the road.

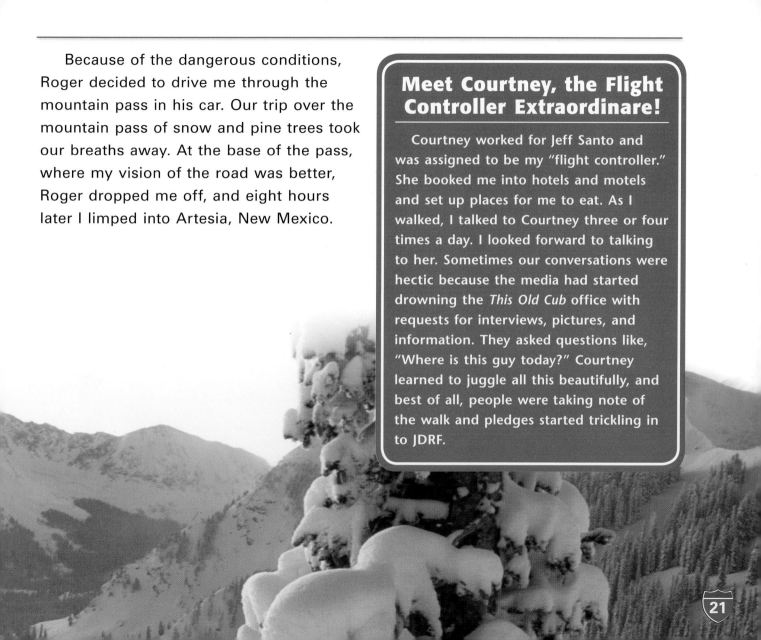

Because of the dangerous conditions, Roger decided to drive me through the mountain pass in his car. Our trip over the mountain pass of snow and pine trees took our breaths away. At the base of the pass, where my vision of the road was better, Roger dropped me off, and eight hours later I limped into Artesia, New Mexico.

Meet Courtney, the Flight Controller Extraordinare!

Courtney worked for Jeff Santo and was assigned to be my "flight controller." She booked me into hotels and motels and set up places for me to eat. As I walked, I talked to Courtney three or four times a day. I looked forward to talking to her. Sometimes our conversations were hectic because the media had started drowning the *This Old Cub* office with requests for interviews, pictures, and information. They asked questions like, "Where is this guy today?" Courtney learned to juggle all this beautifully, and best of all, people were taking note of the walk and pledges started trickling in to JDRF.

When I stopped to rest 20 miles from the Texas border, it was windy and cold. There were bits of cotton everywhere—some of our country's richest cotton fields are planted in this part of the country. In front of me was the only building I'd seen all day. A man named Mr. Brown stepped out from this gigantic barn-like structure and motioned for me to come inside. This was his cotton gin, where loud, roaring compressors processed cotton to be used for clothing. Mr. Brown, impressed by my walk, promised to send a check to JDRF. He filled my water bottle, and I headed down the highway with cotton tufts clinging to my clothes.

This cotton field in New Mexico was covered in cotton. The bits of cotton flew in the air around me and stuck to my clothes.

Texas, Here I Come!

Finally I stepped into Texas and noticed the highways had better road maintenance and wide access roads that ran parallel to the interstate highways—much better for walking! The Texas State Troopers took up where the New Mexico police left off, taking my bag to my next lodging.

On my fourth day in Texas, I walked into Big Spring, Texas, and ate at the Spanish Inn Restaurant, where I met the owners, Nacho and Ada Rodriguez. The place was packed that night, but Nacho had reserved a place for me. We talked baseball while I enjoyed a fantastic dinner. During this two-day rest, Nacho and Ada gave me a tour of Big Spring.

The terrain between Big Spring and Sweetwater, Texas, was filled with grassy plains, oil derricks, rolling hills, and the warmest people I've ever met! Texans are compassionate, fun-loving people, and they love football. In West Texas, where high school football is king, I was about to meet Becky, a football fanatic.

Oil derricks were a common sight in West Texas.

Home of the World's Largest Rattlesnake Round-up!

Hundreds of thousands of people show up every March in Sweetwater, Texas, to watch local people hunt rattlesnakes. The locals use the snake's venom to make medicine that prevents snake-bite deaths. The round-up keeps Sweetwater's notorious rattlesnake population in check and provides a huge celebration for the city each March. Unfortunately I was going to miss this year's round-up by a few weeks.

As I ate breakfast at a local café in Sweetwater, the waitress, Becky, told everyone in the café: "Bill's walked from Arizona and he's going to Chicago." Becky and her husband had never even been outside of Texas. "No need to," she told me. She also never missed a Sweetwater High School Mustangs' football game.

Sweetwater High School is home to the Mustangs.

TEXAS

Becky and her husband, Jeremy, showed me around Sweetwater, and as I left, they said they'd see me again down the road. Within four days, I got a call from Becky and Jeremy, saying they were coming to Abilene, Texas, to have dinner with me.

In Abilene, as I finished up melt-in-your mouth BBQ with them, I noticed tables filled with young men talking baseball. This Michigan junior college team was traveling through Texas for pre-season games. Upon talking with them, I discovered the team's next stop would be St. Louis, Missouri, to play the school that my son pitched for! The team promised to tell Josh that they'd seen me. Things like this happened often; I was in the right spot at the right time, and everywhere I went, the American people's spirit shined.

Abilene, Texas, was where I met a baseball team that would soon be playing against my son's team.

I had an eerie feeling as I sat on the famous "grassy knoll" at Dealey Plaza, the site of John F. Kennedy's assassination.

During my walk through Texas, I slept in both fancy hotels and simple places. It was in Texas where a motel clerk broke down and hugged me, where a hotel owner put my name on the hotel's sign, and where Jeff Santo joined me.

Jeff filmed me walking through Dallas and doing interviews at Dealey Plaza, the site of President John F. Kennedy's assassination in 1963.

In Dallas I was shadowed by helicopters from local television stations, and another wave of spectators stopped to tell me stories of their own battles with diabetes or about family members who had the disease.

My younger brother Bob and his family live in Dallas, so I escaped the motel routine and spent three days relaxing with my feet up and enjoying some home cooking!

My brother Bob welcomed me into his home while I was in Dallas. It was great to stay with family.

Courtney, my "flight controller," continued relaying information about pledges being made to JDRF. One man in Chicago donated $25,000 while others sent in $5 or $10. People dug into their pockets, and I got e-mails from all over. The messages always said, "We're thinking of you! Keep it up!" When I left Dallas and headed for Greenville, Texas, I was well rested.

Sometimes I checked in with Greg Reisig, my friend and cheerleader.

George, the Cubs Fan

While sipping on a power drink at a convenience store in Greenville, Texas, I met an elderly gentleman named George. George was a Cubs fan, yet he had never been to Chicago and had never seen the Cubs play in person. He watched or listened to every game, however.

He told me, "I like the Cubs' style! They always hustle. They don't give up. They always come back! They hustle!"

George was 78, and he promised some day he'd get to Wrigley Field to watch his favorite team. George also had diabetes.

I was so lucky to meet Marilyn on my walk across the country. She was a kind hostess who took great care of me.

From Greenville, Texas, I walked to Whitewright, Texas, the home of Dr. Marilyn Todd-Daniels. Marilyn is an immensely talented artist who lives in a beautiful home full of her artwork. She agreed to take me in, and when I got there, she quickly set about cooking and washing my sweaty clothes. She told me to "bless the land" as I walked—a phrase I remembered for rest of the journey.

Getting a Second Wind in Oklahoma

After a long journey through Texas, I finally crossed another state border and headed north into Oklahoma. In Atoka, Oklahoma, I spent a few hours under a bridge as it hailed hard. When the hail subsided, I made my way to a motel.

That night my college roommate, Mike Murphy, told me that the Cubs wanted me to throw out the first pitch and sing "Take Me Out To The Ball Game" with Ron Santo when I arrived on July 1, 2005, at Wrigley Field! I started getting my second wind and knew I had to finish on time because my friends and family would be waiting!

I walked through Muskogee, Oklahoma, and then on to Wagoner, Oklahoma, where I saw my reflection in a barbershop window and decided it was time for a haircut. The barber had seen me on TV, so she didn't charge me for the haircut. She told me of her father who had died after battling diabetes. I heard the same kind of stories every day.

OKLAHOMA

When I reached Pryor, Oklahoma, I heard the Cubs had won their first game of the season. Film crews from local TV stations continued following me, everyone filming the same thing: me as I walked and pictures of my shoes—always the shoes!

People couldn't believe I'd only worn one pair of shoes for the entire cross-country journey.

Missouri Is Cardinal Country

Once I crossed into Missouri, my friend Carl Mauck called every day, cheering me on and teasing me at the same time: "You won't make it! Better walk 30 miles tomorrow!" He also suggested that I take off my Cubs hat since I was in Cardinal country now. I told him I'd do no such thing because I expected no problems with Cardinal fans even though the Cubs-Cardinals rivalry is fierce.

So there I was in Missouri, with my Cubs hat on, and every town from Joplin to St. Louis greeted me with kindness, although there was some friendly teasing about my Cubs loyalty.

As I hiked through the Ozark Mountains of Missouri, I started seeing the first signs of spring. Everywhere people did double-takes when they saw me; they had likely seen me on TV. Truckers blasted their horns and some even hung out their windows yelling words of encouragement. Whole families set out to search for me in their cars, and the people of Missouri shared their smiles—that's what I'll remember about Missouri—the smiles.

Breakfast On the House

In Cuba, Missouri, after sleeping on a rubber mattress in a vacant cottage the previous night, I went in search of breakfast. There had been many nights on the trip in which sleep didn't come easy regardless of how tired I was, and that past evening had been like that. As I walked into a local coffee shop, I passed out flyers to people and then the good-natured teasing started up between a pack of Cardinal followers and me.

"You're lucky we let you in here!" "How long has it been since the Cubs won a World Series? 97 years? 98 years?" "We got some Cub fans here in town! It's a disease!"

We had some great laughs, and when I got to the counter to pay for my breakfast, the owner smiled at me and said, "No charge, sir. I feel sorry for you Cub fans!" The place roared with laughter.

As I neared St. Louis, the warm May sun felt good. My son waited just ahead, and I was now less than 700 miles from my destination—Wrigley Field.

After a huge hug from Josh, he told me the Michigan baseball team had made a point to find him and take his picture. Josh recalled, "It was the weirdest feeling when I pitched against them, because I knew you bumped into them back in Texas!"

The Gateway Arch is a landmark of St. Louis, Missouri.

I did several fund-raisers while in St. Louis, and the money continued coming in. We were at $160,000, short of our $250,000 goal, but I told Jeff Santo, "Something good's going to happen."

That "something" happened when I met Jim Kelley, a banker from Springfield, Illinois, and Wayne Drehs from ESPN.com.

Jim's son has diabetes, and Jim invited me to go to his home when I reached Springfield, Illinois, to learn what it's like to live with diabetes.

Illinois at Last

Then as I geared up to walk across the Mississippi River, Wayne Drehs from ESPN.com spent a day walking with me. He'd been following the walk for months, and although local television and radio stations had covered the walk, it was now going to be a national story, thanks to Wayne. He sat with me at breakfast in Granite City, Illinois, and asked about my day-to-day routine.

Although I was tired and sore, I remembered all the people I had met and all those who had e-mailed. I told Wayne, "I can almost see the skyscrapers of Chicago from here. I'm close; I'll finish with honor."

Cross-Country Walking Tips

As I walked with Wayne, I explained to him some things that I had learned as a cross-country walker.

1. Face the traffic. On this day we were on the wrong side of the road, walking with the traffic. Within a mile, I was anxious and had a headache. That day's walk was not a good one. When we managed to cross the four-lane highway to the correct side, I immediately felt better, but my routine was off.

2. It's important to rest when your body needs it. Guardrails can be good for a quick rest. The guardrails that are flat on the ends and are not curved are best for sitting.

3. A cross-country walker should be friendly to everyone.

About ten days later, Wayne Dreh's story, "Wild Bill and the Walk Across America," was read by millions of people worldwide on ESPN.com. That was the "something" we had been looking for. From then on, the cell phone never stopped ringing, and I did interviews with radio and television stations from Washington, D.C. to Atlanta, Georgia. Illinois Governor Rod R. Blagojevich even announced he'd walk with me into Wrigley Field and sign a special bill that would help raise funds for diabetes research in Illinois.

The Diabetes Research Check-off Fund Is Created

On July 1, 2005, Governor Rod R. Blagojevich signed legislation that gives Illinois taxpayers a chance to donate money to the state's Department of Human Services, which in turn provides grants for diabetes research.

When I reached Springfield, Illinois, I spent two days with the Kelley family, and I saw the affects diabetes had on their son Andrew, who received insulin shots four times a day. When Andrew's blood sugar was low, he got sleepy and lifeless; when it was high, Andrew was restless. This was what I was walking for—to find a cure for this horrible disease.

As I walked the last few hundred miles through flat prairie land, the weather turned hot, reaching 94–95 degrees Fahrenheit daily!

Children like Andrew who have diabetes must often monitor the amount of sugar in their blood.

My next stop was Bloomington, Illinois, where I showed *This Old Cub* to a standing-room-only audience at a movie theater and spent a few days catching up on much needed sleep.

I also threw out the first pitch at a Peoria Chiefs minor league game in nearby Peoria, Illinois. When one of the Peoria baseball players told me he had diabetes and asked me for **my** autograph, I couldn't speak—here was a player asking a fan for an autograph!

Pete, the Ultimate Cub Fan

I also met Pete who lived in nearby Lincoln, Illinois. Pete has the greatest collection of Cubs memorabilia I've ever seen. His basement is like a Cubs museum with racks of old uniforms on display next to cupboards of autographed baseballs. He even has an old box seat from Wrigley Field. Pete told me that my spirit reminded him of why he was a Cubs fan. It's hard to believe I had that affect on people, all because of this cross-country adventure.

When I reached Pontiac, Illinois, Harry Porterfield, a Chicago news reporter, interviewed me and said that as I got closer to Chicago, things were going to get crazy—everyone was talking about me and Cub fans didn't have much to cheer for except me. Although the Cubs weren't playing well, I knew that on July 1, Wrigley Field would be packed with cheering fans when I walked in.

As I hiked closer to the Chicago suburbs, the traffic was the heaviest I had encountered. From cars whizzing by, there were encouraging shouts and horns blasting away, and some people even turned their cars around, pulling up on my side of the highway to shake my hand and get my autograph.

On June 30, my family greeted me with hugs and tears of happiness as I checked into the Purple Hotel in Chicago's North Shore neighborhood. I thought of Landon Williams, the guy who put me up the first night, along with hundreds of other good, honest people who helped me cross the nation safely. They were back to living their own lives, and here I was, with only six miles left before I walked into Wrigley Field.

When I finally reached Chicago, the Purple Hotel welcomed me to stay the night.

Mission Complete

July 1, 2005, was bright and clear. Photographers were everywhere, helicopters hovered overhead, and people waited at street corners with homemade signs as I walked the final six miles to Wrigley Field.

As I turned onto Addison Street, Carl Mauck, my good friend who had teased me along the way, joined the crowd, saying, "You did it, you crazy man! You did it!"

I replied, "No, we did it!" My army of supporters and I had done it together.

I felt like I had just conquered a climb to the highest mountaintop and now I was on top of the world—what a feeling!

July 1, 2005 was declared "Wild Bill Holden Day" in Illinois.

I took my final steps of the walk on the greenest, most beautifully kept lawn in the country—Wrigley Field. As a gate in right field opened, 40,000 people rose up in a thunderous roar, and I made my way to the infield where Ron Santo waited to greet me. We met and hugged, both of us with tears in our eyes.

My first pitch bounced into Cubs' pitcher Kerry Wood's glove about two feet short of home plate, but nobody booed me for the bad pitch. The fans were just happy that I had completed the trip.

Singing "Take Me Out to the Ball Game" with Ron Santo during the 7th inning stretch topped the whole day off. I had just finished walking 2,100 miles in 172 days! Thousands of cars and trucks had whizzed past every day, and I had walked through rain, snow, sleet, hail, and unbelievable heat.

My name is Bill Holden, and I walked across America!

The walk to Chicago raised over $250,000 for JDRF, and I saw the best of America: her people and their spirits!

Time Line of Bill Holden's Walk

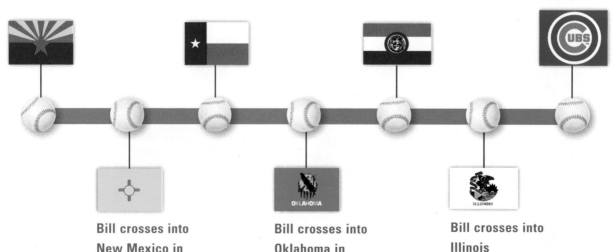

Bill begins the walk on January 11, 2005, in Prescott Valley, AZ.

Bill crosses into Texas in mid-February-early March.

Bill crosses into Missouri in early May.

Bill walks into Wrigley Field on July 1, 2005.

Bill crosses into New Mexico in late January.

Bill crosses into Oklahoma in mid-April.

Bill crosses into Illinois in late May.